Pressed Flowers and the Sea Serpent

Michaela Belmont

Pressed Flowers and the Sea Serpent

Copyright © 2022 by Michaela Belmont.

All rights reserved. This book or any portion thereof may not be reproduced or used in any manner whatsoever without written permission of the author except for the use of brief quotations in a book review.

First Edition 2022.

ISBN: 978-0-9995726-6-5 (Paperback)
ISBN: 978-0-9995726-7-2 (Ebook)

Library of Congress Control Number: 2022909425

Requests for permission or further information can be sent to info@michaelabelmont.com.

Cover image used under license from Shutterstock.com (artist Andrew Ostrovsky).

www.michaelabelmont.com.

Light shines through me like panes of glass.
Both the light and the dark.

Table of Contents

Opening Letter

Gold and Blue Flowers in the Meadow
- 1   Transform
- 2   Healer
- 3   Erupted
- 5   Razzle Dazzle
- 7   Parakeets
- 8   Send Love
- 9   Stardust – Light and Dark
- 10   What We Believe
- 11   Be Willing to Walk Away
- 12   Winter Morning
- 13   Beautiful Things Collected
- 14   I Am
- 15   Sun and Moon
- 16   Here and the Dream
- 17   Unbridled Measure
- 18   Shattering
- 19   Faint Beginning
- 20   The Edge of the World
- 21   Alive
- 22   The Next Version of Me
- 24   Flock of Butterflies
- 26   Peace

Melancholia, Land of Grayscale
- 29   Yet
- 30   Shadow Mouths
- 31   Once-Empire
- 32   Intersection
- 33   The Dreamscapes
- 34   Astronaut
- 35   The Light

36 Wanted to Tell You
37 Father's Day
38 Out of Lack
39 Seagull
40 Picking at Wounds
41 Luminescent Flower
42 Snow-Covered Cabin
43 Healthy Anger
45 Everything in Motion
46 Art in the Apocalypse
47 On Starting Over
48 One of My Harshest Teachers
49 Closed Off

Old Blood the Color of Rust

53 Namaryllaryne
54 The Perpetual Night: Firelight
55 Entreaty of the Demons (to Her of the Bleeding Feet)
57 Monster Inside
58 Beasts
59 A Sickness in My Head
60 Deconstruction
61 Black Void
62 Soul-Death
63 Mausoleum of Dust
64 Shining Path
65 The Macabre Club and the Snake Men Servers
66 Coiled Inside
67 Ancient
68 Hate and Healing

The Ancient Forests

73 Epochs
74 Landfall
75 Tarot
76 Tower
77 Love of Lives Past

- 79   For F., Again
- 80   The Queen in the Forest
- 81   Jeweled Wings
- 82   The Castle of Winding Things
- 83   Apology, Finally

Of Storms and the Sea
- 87   Pressed Flowers and the Sea Serpent
- 89   A Fisher by the Sea
- 91   The Mermaids and the Moon
- 93   The Storm
- 94   Two Souls Out at Sea
- 95   Hollow of the River
- 96   Consciousness
- 97   Sunset Over the Sea
- 99   Mistress of Her Vessel
- 100   The Wires

About the Author

OPENING LETTER

I. SOUL-CURRENT

This is something of a preface, I suppose. Either that or it's an essay, or a collection of disparate musings. The linear fallacy that I used to accept once led me to assume that as I wrote more books and published them it would become easier. "Practice makes perfect" as they say, and so I thought as more books were birthed from my heart into this world their introductions, afterwords, descriptive text and whatnot would eventually spill out easily from my mind and coil themselves, elegantly shaped, onto the paper.

But it seems that this commonsense assumption, like just about every other one that I have been told, doesn't play out so neatly in practice. In reality I find the deeper the things I have to say, the more amorphous, intuitive, and colorfully, obtusely shapeless they choose to become. It would seem that the more fluently I write in emotion the more I struggle to write in words. It's a strange thing.

I wonder if it is perhaps indicative of a deeper exhaustion I have: the overwhelming sense of bone-tiredness that sinks down inside whenever I feel as though I'm supposed to perform, impress, explain. Our whole lives we're expected to construct ourselves into productive, socially acceptable narratives, and be able to switch the masks at a moment's notice based on the company we're in. Sometimes we wear the masks so well we don't even know we're wearing them. But I'm so tired of the struggle to be anyone other than myself at this point. So tired of wielding anything in my life that I am not meant for, that is not meant for me. I don't want to fight against the soul-current. I want a life that I am aligned with, one that is also looking for me.

II. TRANSFORM

I went through some of the darkest nightmares that exist, and I went through them alone. But that has given me the power to heal deep spiritual wounds, to transform darkness and toxicity into beauty and meaning. I can handle the raw energy and emotion that permeates the world and universe. It makes sense. When we overcome hardship - climb the mountain, defeat the dragon, weather the storm - we gain gifts, or perhaps unlock the ones that were already within us.

Pressed Flowers and the Sea Serpent is my latest endeavor to transform emotion and personal experience into cathartic meaning. It is divided into five sections, each corresponding with different emotional, spiritual, and cognitive landscapes. Whether I am diving into the depths of sparking, neon-colored clouds of personal imagination or opening a far-flung cosmic door into the universal infinite is uncertain. Perhaps it is both of these things.

III. BELIEVE

As you grow internally, you're able to expand out further in kindness and tolerance. You're able to hold space for more perspectives than just your own, or just those similar to your own. You can see the underlying feelings and needs uniting all of humanity, hidden though they are by wildly disparate behaviors and belief systems. You can evolve your understanding and develop forgiveness, both for yourself and others. You learn how to process and release pain as you grow more confident in knowing when to reach out to people, and when to let them go. And most of all, you're able to expand your consciousness and free your soul by letting go of your constraining singular identity.

I consider it my greatest test in this world to keep believing in the beauty and nobility of people, no matter how much evidence I am given to the contrary. I try to keep in mind that people are sacred, even when they do not do the same for me. I try to remember that they are sacred even if they have forgotten.

IV. CURE

I used to think that the ills of the world were something I could solve. That I could cure the worst in people and set the world aright.

But these things have always been here, and always will be. At least as long as there are people.

Those who dream of ruling the world are trying desperately to hold onto handfuls of sand in their clenched fists. Delusions of grandeur. But equally deluded are those who dream of creating a utopia. (I say this as someone who has struggled with fantasies of doing just that.) You cannot dispense happiness and high values to those who have not yet found those concepts inside themselves. You cannot hand others enlightenment any more than you can claim dominion over them. Power over others is a lie, transient and slippery, a serpent that is as likely to coil back and strike its wielder as it is to do as commanded. Your control over others ends the moment they recognize it for the falseness that it is. Whether it be chains in your left hand or bread in your right, it is an illusory spell that is broken the moment someone says its name.

Power cultivated internally is the only kind that's real. That is the power, the essence, that grounds you and frees you at the same time. You are neither crusader nor tyrant, neither victim nor child. You have true strength in that you are whole, with no need for others to complete you or play out certain dynamics with you.

I cannot save the world, nor conquer it if I wished to. I cannot solve it like a math problem. What I can do is outgrow it. I can transcend it. I can embody kindness, and love, and try to help and heal where I can. And whatever intent I try to create in the world will also create a mirrored effect in me.

V. INTEGRITY

After saying all of that, I will make an appeal to humanity.

As a species we are perpetually learning and exploring the fringes of our understanding. We are always creating new technologies and evolving.

But what I have found to be the most important is what kind of people we are while we are doing these things. It is the integrity, compassion, and wisdom with which we move through this world that matters most. Advanced human-esque robots, the colonization of other planets, and cities that hang in the sky are without merit if it is a callous, cruel, and senseless society that builds them. As important as technological and economic development are ethical and spiritual development – the exploration of heart and soul. I care as much about the evolution of our species' ethics and kindness as I do about any other facet of our evolution. I would argue that it is actually the most important. Let us become a species that does not have to hide its face in its hands out of shame for the things it has done; let us not be a species that slams down its fist out of frustration for not understanding why its actions have the effects that they do. Let us be deep thinkers; let us be deep feelers. Let us be Awake.

VI. WHOLENESS

Determination and hope well up inside me when I watch the traumas I thought I would never get over drift away into the distance, fading over time to small, barely perceptible blips on the horizon.

Of course, they're not always gone. Some days I wake and all those things are wrapped around my throat, as real and alive as the day they were born, suffocating me and filling my eyes with blood. Another definition for CPTSD, I believe, should be "that which keeps the ghosts alive." The dead still walking.

And yet after so many years of healing, tears, and brave, good choices, I find myself most days standing upon a peaceful mountain summit. On those days I watch the old pains fade away.

The beautiful truth revealed, the blissful panacea, the ultimate relief, is this: it is never too late for your life to start. The one you really wanted. No matter the agonies to which you have been subjected, your soul and the light within you are stronger. They are able to absorb it all, and transform it. You can explore both the daylight and midnight aspects of yourself, your life and your past, and know that you will not be wrenched apart by the discovery. Though you may have, through pain, disillusionment, or trauma, lost pieces of your wholeness, you have the ability to renew. You have always contained within you the power to heal and become whole once more. You have the resilience, courage, and heart to traverse the endless landscapes inside yourself, and emerge on the other side.

VII. ETERNAL

I would like to share a truth that I have found in life. Every experience, every achievement, every relationship, begins, proceeds, and then ends like the seasons. Nothing is permanent. In spite of all my grasping, all of my efforts, all that I have been able to reach and hold eventually turns to ash in my hands. I watch it blow away over the sea, carried by the wind into the sunset as the waves push and pull against the sands below.

I know I had a different name, once. I was eternal and infinite; all that I loved loved me, and indeed was part of me. We were all part of each other. There was no loneliness, no cold, no distance. Someday I will wake, and remember my true name.

Someday I will go home, and all the hurts will just be memories. Memories that, sooner or later, will turn into dust and be blown away on the wind. And I will be so overcome by joy that I will not miss them.

Michaela Belmont
5/6/22

Gold and Blue Flowers in the Meadow

Transform

There are pure, vivid flowers that grow
from the soil of released secrets and suffering.
Take your pain, your shame,
and plant it back into the earth from where it came.
It will grow into something transformed and new.
Let me remind you.

A truth you once knew
and then forgot.
A truth you walked away from.
The understanding that the point
of agony, of misery, of everything ugly
is so that you can plant it
into the ground, into the ocean
and witness the most beautiful things bloom.

Healer

I am still standing
after the betrayal by the one I loved the most.
I wear a crown of red petals and thorns,
and blood runs down my throat
and front from where his claws gouged me.
It changed me, and when I speak
grief speaks
also.

But that's not all there is to me.
When I hold out my hands, dirtied waters run clean
and green life springs anew from charred earth.
It took a ripping open of all my deepest wounds,
a sundering and a rebirth,
to understand that I am a healer.

Erupted

It was the event that killed me, broke me
and awoke me.
The person that happened to
is no longer alive.
The earth cracked apart, and with
a wrenching screech
the lava erupted in pouring agony.
It seemed like it would never stop.
This sickening vomiting of eons of repressed pain.
But it did finally stop.

Years have gone by.
I can now stand at a distance, behind the low fence
and observe this monument, this preserved time in history.
The time it all ripped open
and the skies darkened with ash
for eons.

But at the end, I reflect, wind blowing in my hair,
after it all came out, there was a freshness to the air
and renewed joy in the wildlife
and the reappearance of flowers I hadn't seen
since I was a child.
Sometimes it takes the ugliest experiences
to cleanse out that which was buried under.
It had been stunting the growth
of everything.
At a certain point, everything began
to rot.

Now things grow
in me.
Now my landscape responds to me, to my touch,
instead of shuddering away like one does

from an absentee mother.
Now I feel my home in me,
and know my body belongs to me,
not to those who want to own it
or cause it pain.
I don't belong to those who have hurt me,
nor to those who have ignored my suffering.

I belong solely to myself.

Razzle Dazzle

I went back to an animal rescue at which I used to volunteer
and spent time with the cats in back again.
The ward's name is "Catnip". All felines contained within
are unadoptable to the public.
I found Dazzle, an old orange tabby
who, once roused from his sleep
looked very happy to see me.
I was happy to see him too.

As I made the rounds, petting all the cats that would have me,
I reflected on the nature of kindness, and of the fact
that we don't seem capable of a meaningful depth of it
until we have been broken apart.
It is only when we hold our own broken pieces
that we are able to hold those of others,
as well as the world's.
I spent an hour with cats the rest of the world
wouldn't bother to look twice at.

I tried to adopt Dazzle two months ago.
They wouldn't allow it because they said he's a sprayer.
Adopting out sprayers to volunteers had gone badly for them
in the past.

Sometimes rules and regulations get in the way.
When I was younger, how I used to rail against them.
But sometimes they're there to protect you.
If the rules had been followed better
perhaps I wouldn't have had my insides ripped out
by a man I thought I could trust more than anyone.
So sometimes fences are the things
that heartfelt rebellion was made for.
But other times they're there to keep you
from being hurt by what you love.

And from hurting what you love.
Maybe visiting Dazzle, and Bear, and Archie at the rescue
is better than Dazzle learning what it's like to have a home,
only to lose it and be brought back in tragedy.

I sit with Dazzle quietly with the lights turned off,
the winter afternoon sun coming in through the windows.
Catnip is quiet
and I'm the only human on the floor.
I reflect on kindness, and broken pieces.
I reflect on the necessity of boundaries
in love.

Parakeets

A cute sideways turn of the head,
sweet, coy little blinks
and just like that
I have made friends with two parakeets
at the pet store.
We can speak the same language, no words necessary.
And again, I am delightfully reminded
of our sameness, despite our different bodies.
In their bright eyes I saw Truth, and I think
they saw the same in mine.
They are little people, little blue and green people
and even if humans terrify me some more today,
as they often do
I still have made connections today.

Send Love

If all the trials I have been through in this life
have taught me anything, it's that
love is the answer to everything.
Send love to everyone.
Send love even to your enemies.
Love will erode and wipe away
everything else.

Stardust: Light and Dark

I am infinitely powerful.
I am a limitless witch, god, faerie.
I am an infinitely powerful cosmic being
made of stardust and light, both the bright
warm light of the day and the searing neon
born of stars exploding and planets colliding in the dark.

Light shines through me like panes of glass.
Both the light and the dark.

What We Believe

We build what we believe.
So let us dream a better world
into being.

Be Willing to Walk Away

In order to get the love you want,
you have to be willing to walk away
from everything that isn't it.

You must be willing to walk away
from everything that is less than you deserve.

Winter Morning

There is a special comfort
in the dark womb of a dark room
at 6:30 on a winter morning
from whose blankets you never want
to be removed from.

There is a darkness that cradles us in time,
not just in space,
and when these moments come
I know I have gone back
to when these feelings first began.
Back to when my eyes and hands were new
and my fear and love were too.

Beautiful Things Collected

I am a little weathered, a little worse for wear.
I tire easily, and I'm often sad.
But look at all the beautiful things I have collected
in this life.

It was all I ever wanted.
To discover beautiful things
in the midst of all the ugliness
and apathy.

****

I have traveled on this road called life
for what feels like a very long time.
I will likely be on it for an even longer time to come.
Over the years I have walked through some of the worst storms,
nightmare storms that lasted for decades.
I have seen humanity's apathy in the face
of suffering and soul destruction
and I have seen the monsters that rise
out of the decay in people's hearts.
I have seen the monster feeding
in the dark shadows
of my own heart.

But I have seen some beautiful things too. I have, I have.

I Am

I am the wind blowing through the trees;
I am the warm daylight settling down on closed eyelids.
I am the songbird perched on the branch;
I am the infant laughing in the distance.

I am water;
I am the waterfall.
I am music;
I am the song.

Sun and Moon

"Masculine." "Feminine." Irrelevant.
I contain both the Sun and the Moon inside,
churning out pressure and radiating energy
and pushing and pulling the tides.

Here and the Dream

A long time ago, a bridge
connecting two floating halves was broken,
the two landmasses left ever separated
in the void.
This whole life has been a fervent journey
to build a bridge again across the abyss
and travel
home
again.

Here and the dream.
Here and the other.

Unbridled Measure

If you want to wish someone ill, wish them only to keep living.
If you want to wish them happiness, wish them the same.
For life contains both agony and joy in abundance,
unbridled measure.

Shattering

When you start off born,
everything's free and slowly moving.
A thick, glittering substance
with structure yet to be formed.

As you grow older the liquid takes shape.
It becomes
Solid Form.
And then as the blocks build up on each other,
the construct takes shape -
but as it grows taller it
hardens.

That's not necessarily bad.
If things didn't solidify they couldn't grow and expand.
Couldn't become more
intricate.
But it does mean that the bad parts, the toxic and sick –
they get solidified in there too,
and become just about impossible
to remove.
It takes a shattering then.
A trauma so agonizing, a true horror
to smash this thing down to the ground.
But therein, the opportunity to build up
something healthier than before.

Faint Beginning

When it all crumbled and collapsed before my eyes
I thought it was the end.
Then the blooming came and I thought that I had been wrong,
and mistaken a beginning for an end.
Now I know it was in fact the end, and I had spent the years after
roaming across the scorched landscape as it recovered.
And now, on the edge of the horizon,
I think I see the beginning.

The Edge of the World

I cannot believe I ever thought
that another person had the power to heal
my pain, or give me the answers I needed.

I journeyed to the edge of the world
and found myself waiting there.

Alive

For so long I ran from the love I felt,
from the betrayals and heartbreaks that had occurred,
from the pieces of me I thought had died.
But now I realize that all of those feelings
prove that I'm alive.
There are people who are truly dead inside.
Numb, shaken dead or never awakened.
As long as I can feel something,
even sad or used or ripped apart -
that means something in me hasn't hardened,
something in me hasn't died.

I have not forgotten
how to feel.
That's how I know I'm alive.

The Next Version of Me

The next version of me
won't be one who writes sad poetry.
She will be riding wild on the wind
and howling with joyous savagery.
She will be free, with jagged black tattoos
on one side of her jaw
and ragged old scars on the other.

The next version of me
will barely remember this version of me.
Will hardly recall the shame, the pain
and all the betrayals and misunderstandings
that got her to where she will be.
Will look back laughing on all the time spent
secretly yearning for those who destroyed me
to come back
and say they were sorry.
To say that they loved me.

The next version of me
won't be the type that yearns
at all.
She will represent the spirit and strength
that others yearn for.
She will curl her fingers around the horse's mane,
around the motorcycle's handlebars,
and ride off howling
with delight.

I am willing to die
so that she can be.
This is a first.
All of the older versions of me died violently,
screams wrenching from their throats,

fingers leaving bloody trails
and fingernails
on the linoleum floors
and the trim on doorframes.
They were miserable and abused
but still, still …
they wanted to live.

They didn't want to die, and so
they did not go gracefully when it was their time
and even now I find I've been clinging on
to the corpse of the previous me inside,
her love, and her pain,
instead of just letting her die.
It will go differently this time.
I will let myself die when the next version of me
is ready to come striding out into the light.
And riding fervently off
into the night.

Flock of Butterflies

Once we were in the darkness,
sleeping, silenced, and hurt.
We were trapped in
the half-remembered conversations
and distorted perceptions of other people.
They contained us within their pens,
their barbed tongues,
their strategic memories.
We were trapped
in jars
in rooms
in handcuffs.

They told us we were cockroaches.
Of no use to them or anyone.
In their shallow chasing of immediate needs,
they could not see the shadows
of the brilliant wings we would someday possess,
held tightly against our bodies.

But then we Awoke.
We remembered our worth.
We opened our mouths and Spoke.
We took pens in our own hands and Wrote.
And we changed the whole story.

They called us cockroaches,
not realizing that we were caterpillars,
that we would one day
be butterflies.

Much time has passed.
We have suffered, and learned, and grown, and loved.
We have shed the old skin and have nothing left to fear.

We are miraculous, a prophecy foretold.
We are a flock of butterflies lighting up the sky.

Peace

Peace is a small, furry thing,
with sweet eyes and soft wings
that flutters a bit ahead,
then lands and looks back
to see if you will follow.

Contentment is a neighborhood path
on a pleasant spring day, with purple,
pink, and white-blossomed trees
adorning the way on either side.

The Light doesn't roar. It doesn't perform
or otherwise try to catch your attention.
It is only the dance of bees, the sounds
of birds and squirrels.
If you are not still you could miss it.

Heaven doesn't dance or pull out all the bells and whistles.
It does not proceed with extravagant parades.
It is simply a warm, sunny day
where things are full and whole.

Melancholia,
Land of Grayscale

Yet

Two people are talking.
One says, "I do have a tendency to idealize people,
that's true. It's nice having things to believe in."

The other then asks, "But who are *you*?"

A wry smile from the first speaker, then:
"I am a bird that doesn't know it's a bird, yet.
A tree that doesn't know it's a tree, yet.
A song that doesn't know it's a song,
yet."

Shadow Mouths

The three shadow branches on the wall
gained mouths and spoke to me.
Or at least about me.
My eyes were open, but I couldn't stir.
Finally I could move and they stopped
talking.

I turned my head to the pillow and saw
a small, tightly woven spark of energy.
It was all jagged, curly lines radiating outward.
I awoke, turned my head,
and saw the little spider;
this time
in the physical
plane.

Once-Empire

I walk through sanitized white rooms, lined with gold leaf
past a horned man taking the dais
of a place I've forgotten the name of.
Wandering the halls of a once-empire
now looted, its name lost to time and space.

Intersection

In a dream I saw a cardboard sign fluttering
across an intersection, fluttering corner after corner.
Soon after I saw the tanned homeless man
who had held it racing out to get it, shirtless,
long hair like a mane and dark eyes like a panicked horse.
The scream was never born in my throat.
There was no time
and in that moment the formerly still intersection
rumbled to life, cars barreling 50 miles an hour
and the worst part is that as they plunged
forward on and by I saw that they had no drivers inside.
Just line after line of blank windshields
and staring headlight eyes
and though I woke without seeing
what I knew would occur
I knew he reminded me of Jesus, as Jesus would surely look
in this day and age – or in any day and age.
Disheveled, yet noble, so fervently alive
lost in a dead world with panic in his eyes
wondering in his last moments
why no one would stop.

The Dreamscapes

Bleeding trees and possessed queens,
juxtaposed with intimate betrayal
and the learning of self-respect
and personal accountability.
Opening one's eyes to a greater responsibility
for the world in which one lives.
Emerging from the dreamscapes,
simultaneously joyful and nightmarish
into the harsh, dusty
World.

Astronaut

I looked at you and saw an astronaut, with whom I could have ventured
across the icy depths of the solar system
to see with our own eyes Jupiter's storming Red Spot
and Saturn's countless spinning rings.
I believed you contained within
all of the wonders that I had not yet been able to reach,
that your thumbs had flicked across the pages
of magick texts that I had forgotten,
that you could remind me of what they were
but in truth your eyes were as lost and unseeing as mine were,
your compass every bit as broken,
and when your grasping hands grappled with my heart's cliff face
and broke pieces off, and you and they fell, all screaming –
I was too young a God to feel for your mistake,
too consumed by my own grief
to leave some flowers there,
a memorial for you that would say
Here was a mortal, a man
that tried.

The Light

I dream of feeling better
the way a soul plunged into darkness,
surrounded by concrete and nothing else
reaches out to the light
near the ceiling.
Coming in from that small window,
a feeble warm ray of daylight, a hope,
a wishing, a dream.
I have hope the way an imprisoned elephant
reaches its trunk up towards the light.

Wanted to Tell You
what we all wish we could say
and what we wish would be said to us.

There's something I wanted to tell you.
Something I wanted to say
that would make all the pain go away.
Something that would reassure you
that I was not trying to hurt you,
not trying deliberately to be cruel.

There was something I wanted to tell you
that would reassure you
that this was not a game.
Not a lie.
That would prove to you
that I'm just damaged and dumb
and that I make mistakes sometimes
but that I love you.

I want more than anything to say it to you.

Father's Day

I was weeping on the bathroom floor again today.
I'll be thirty in September, though for the past hour I was two.
Those howling animal sounds, inhuman, grieving,
muffled as best they could be
by my hands so tired of carrying
everything.

"Please take care of me," I sobbed to a father long since gone,
who humiliated and betrayed me and got away with it all.
"Please take care of me."
And as the wailing sounds of loss filled up past my throat,
and as my head pounded with grief almost three decades old,
as I spun out of control across space and across time,
I thought:

'This is a part of me that needs to die.
It's time.'

Out of Lack

This understanding comes to me,
slithering as a delicate silver snake,
that my art comes from the empty spaces
between what should have happened
and what did happen.
From that longing for what I wish I had done
and what I wish I hadn't.

I know now that my inspiration comes from
the dark places that never burst into light.
That never took root and grew life.
My art comes from causing
beauty and meaning to grow out of decay.
Out of lack.

Like the skilled spider crafting in the shadows
I will weave intricate, golden, unrivalled tapestries.
I will create all of the magnificent somethings
out of nothing.

Seagull

A dreary winter afternoon somewhere between
That lady doesn't like me, I need to try harder
and
It all hurts so much I need to die
I'm stopped at a red light watching a gull
perch picturesque against the cloudy sky.
The color scheme is front of me is shades of black, white, and gray
and I see that near the seagull standing on the stoplight's highest point
is a traffic camera, coiled coyly
and I think to myself, *surely there's a metaphor here*
but I can't think of it.

Picking at Wounds

That's what you always do.
You feel a pimple, and instead of letting it rise
and then fall, a small bump, as pimples do
you pick it apart, turn it into a wound.
And then you call it truth.

Sometimes bad things happen.
They rise and they fall.
But some of them, they could have stayed
small.
Until you picked them apart.
And then pulled off the scab.
Over and over and over again.
Marring an otherwise lovely face
that you couldn't perceive at all.

Luminescent Flower

Years ago I met the one, the one I had
                      been waiting
my entire life to meet.
He broke me almost immediately.

For those few minutes before, I knew
                      how it felt
to be truly connected to a human being.
The feeling of having found
another member of my species.
For a few blissful eternities
I wasn't alone.

This life will go on longer.
I will keep evolving and unfurling,
a blossom truly unlike any other in the
        world.
But I will always be alone.
Whether because there are no others
                      like me
or because I cannot bear to let anyone
        near me,
I will be alone.
I will be the single silken luminescent
        flower
blooming in the dark.

Snow-Covered Cabin

My pain will be my company,
my comfort and my home.

No one will ever find me nestled inside
this snow-covered cabin
down the unending winding road.

No one will ever reach me here.
Or be able to hurt me.

Healthy Anger

I let my anger lean into me
and share what it wants to say.
I'm so angry my boundaries were violated.
I'm so angry you didn't treat me better.
I'm so angry I didn't feel seen or heard by anyone
when I tried to talk about it.
I'm so angry I didn't feel understood.
I'm angry is better than *I hate you*
because *I hate you* is an externalization,
a distraction from what is going on inside me.
I hate you gives you all my power.
I'm angry tells me vitally important things about *me*.
And what *I* need.

Until just a few years ago, I never let anger free at all
because the feeling was sickly tied with powerlessness.
When my father was abusing me, getting angry with him
only caused him to hurt me worse.
And getting angry with the other adults in my life
for not doing something about him
only caused them to scapegoat me more.
She's so moody, they would say.
So belligerent and immature.

But I am entitled to my anger. It is a part of me.
It is what tells me when I am being mistreated.
Keeping it muted all those years
only helped me find friendships and relationships
that reincarnated the pain and disrespect.
The kind of people who call you profanities
and then point their finger in your face
and tell you it was your fault that they talked to you that way.
People who put their unwanted hands on your body
and then laugh when you pull away.

People who toss you their scraps
and expect you to be grateful.

Some days I feel like I love you,
weep over you and miss you,
and other days I feel like I hate you
as just one more person who broke a piece off of me
and walked away.
But the underlying cause of these situations is always the same.
When I deny my anger, I set myself up
for betrayal.

Everything in Motion

You build monuments, raise them,
sail away and then mourn them,
not realizing that even if you were able to return
to that exact spot in which they were constructed,
they wouldn't be there anymore.

Time marches on, everything is in motion,
and that which you grieve isn't etched in stone
awaiting your return.
It was moving away as fast as you were,
and now, trust me …
there is nothing there to return to.

Art in the Apocalypse

As I'm leaving work, it seems the parking lot
is the only landmass in a world of fog.
The bad air, the constant fires.
California's on fire.
We all wear masks due to the plague,
and the locusts and murder hornets have come.

Why does the art stir in me as the ash consumes it all?
As it spirals down white to coat our clothes,
our eyelashes, the fur of our pets.
Why do I feel so fervent in the apocalypse?
How can I be so alive in the middle of hell?

The moon is resting crimson
on a bed of pitch violet tonight.
Beneath her eldritch light all of us,
bizarre configurations of atoms and cells that we are,
crawl to and fro on the dark alien world below,
coughing in the smog.

On Starting Over

I was happier then, for a while.
Because things were better than they had ever been before.
But sadness followed me out through the door
and as freedom began to fall on my lips
in such an expected, mundane way
the same old grief settled on my eyes

            weighing down my heart.

One of My Harshest Teachers

Thank you for showing me how threadbare I was.
How exposed to the elements I was after so many years
of heavy rain and fabric tearing.
Your rough handling tore me apart,
when I should have been able to shrug it off.

I should have only felt a bit repulsed and hurt
and then gone on my way.
But after so many injuries and years left to the weather
I was more fragile than I ever could have imagined.
It took a heartbreak shattering my brittle core
for me to see that I could be more.
That I deserved
more.

You walked into my house of grief
and I thought you were the answer.
And, in a way,
I suppose you were.
Thank you for showing me
that I deserved
more.

Closed Off

I retreat to cry.
I hide to grieve.
Always have I drawn behind door, behind curtain
in order to wear my grief.
These tarnished strings of pearls and scarves.
Because in the past when I would tell others
that I had been hurt, they did not believe
and the agony cut me down
to the core of my being.
Down to the bone and muscle.
So I learned young how to retreat,
how to hide pain and how to hide inside my grief.
Because if no one knows about it they can't invalidate,
say they don't believe.
No one can dismiss my grief
if they don't know about it.

Seemingly a coincidence, though it is not –
I have spent my life alone.
Isolated, haunted, wandering this empty moor
with its crumbling cemeteries and towers.
Spending my years wandering
and wondering why I feel so alone.

When he hurt me, I ran with my shame to those I loved
and wept and threw my pain onto the floor.
I wanted them to hold me close
and wipe tears from my eyes
and tell me it was going to be okay.
I wanted them to tell me it wasn't my fault.
I wanted them to be angry with him.

But they drew back and away.
They talked amongst themselves.

Quietly.
And then they stopped talking. It was over.
And as I saw their fading backs
and heard the click of the door

I saw I was the one who had been shut out.

Old Blood the Color of Rust

Namaryllaryne
[nama-rilla-ryne]

There is a blood-red castle on the cliff
overhanging the thrashing sea.
When asked of it all shudder and answer in kind:
"That is the cursed house of the damned -
Namaryllaryne."

Forever it has stood, and forever it will stand,
housing all of those lost and betrayed
by a trusted one's hand.
Inside in darkness stalk cursing figures,
tragic apparitions using ghostly lanterns to see.
They howl and cry out and gnash their teeth in rage,
searching for those who have wronged them
or those they have lost along the way.
You will sometimes hear their screams from inside:
"Oh God, please release us
from Namaryllaryne."

The manipulations, rapes, murders, genocides
that have taken place throughout the ages.
These atrocities don't ever die.
Their anguish and hate forevermore will find
a home in the blood-red castle
of Namaryllaryne.

The Perpetual Night: Firelight

The woman who pulled down the sky
and made it dark.
The period of Perpetual Night
during which those who preyed on others
would be held responsible.
Punished.
Made to suffer.

Demons roamed through the landscape
and through her blood.
She and they danced amidst the corpses,
shadows vicarious against the walls
struck by blood and lit by firelight.

Her frame grew tall and skeletal, her eyes became black holes.
Those who fought against her
said she had become a monster herself.
A twisted caricature of all she believed in.
But she knew that this was the only way
that those who had betrayed her would be held accountable.
No more would she have to hear that she should just forgive,
that the crimes committed against her weren't really that terrible.
No. Her rage, her hate, would never be made docile.
Her anguish would never subside.
It would grow, and crest, and swell,
and consume all who remained in its path.

She would not be small or silent. Not anymore.
She would feast on their monstrous flesh
and then swallow the moon.

Entreaty of the Demons (to Her of the Bleeding Feet)

It is time for you to claim your throne,
your crown, your royal title!
The one that was always yours,
you had only to walk the path of thorns and fire
to reach it.

We are ready to receive you!
And, most importantly, you are now ready, too.
We are here to serve you –
Blood Queen.

Lead us to joy, to power, to the eternal flame!
With you at the helm our brilliance will never fade.
The dead will rise and walk for you,
the animals will roar and fight for you.
Dams will burst, storms will batter the earth.
Demons, your legion, will climb out
of the walls into the mortal world, at your call.
Spirits will share their gifts and insights,
plants will blossom and vine at your touch.

And – most importantly of all –
no man of earth will ever again be able to hurt you.
You have surpassed them in power and strength.
They will not be able to touch you.
Even your father – naught but a frail, pale shadow
in the firebright illumination of your magnificence.

Just say war, and it shall be so!
Seeds of fire, of hail, of disease, of snow.
Whatever the Blood Queen desires
she has the power to make so.

We are ready to receive you,

to receive your blessing
and place upon you your crown.
You will always have company in the Great Hall;
you will always have someone to hold hands with
and dance with in the ballroom.
You will never feel alone or frightened
again.

Long may you reign!
Blood Queen!

Monster Inside

I am well aware of the monster inside.
It stalks inside every one of us.
While I envy those who have never met theirs,
wearing those wide decent eyes,
I trust those like me more -
lips hardened into a thin line,
eyes tired and wise.
Tired from knowing and wrestling down a fiend.
Always keeping it in line.
As we walk through society,
among the peaceful sheep
who haven't seen the things we've seen.
Who haven't met the things
we've met.

Beasts
self-loathing

What foul, lascivious beast is this
that brings out the worst in man.
That turns him from a doctor and loving father
into a slathering monster.

What filthy sacks decorate this cliff face,
what creases down below
draw a human's eye and contort them,
sicken them, into black-eyed beasts
from whose mouths the panting waters flow.
And the filthy verbose flowers grow.

What kind of beast is this
to bring about a man's apocalypse
and change him from loving, funny, kind
into everything I despise
and deserve.

A Sickness in My Head

There is a sickness in my head
that tells me they only want me for my body.
That they want to know me in their bed
but not in any other way.
Not as a human being.

There is a sickness in my head.

There is a corruption in my soul
that says my emotions and thoughts
are 'too much.'
That my needs are an all-consuming black hole
that they will always run away from.

There is a ghoul standing behind me
who tells me that I need to die.
When I turn to see her she looks just like me
except for the rotten hair and screaming void
for eyes and mouth.
She tells me they could never care about me.

There is a sickness in my head.
Though I live in green gardens these days,
with loving friends and devoted pets,
abusers faded away into the past,
still this darkness nests inside me
a mass resting on my head, weighing it
down
growing into my spine.
I am somehow a different, toxic ecosystem
separate from all that around me.
Yet the bees still try
to visit.

Deconstruction

I have to tell you a secret.
I have felt ruined so many times,
defaced and disgraced,
that I have had to dismantle the concept
of being ruined and broken apart.
The idea of having some pure pearl or innocent light
that must be zealously held onto.
I have had to pull apart the paradigm
of clean and light versus corrupted and whore
simply because there is no way I could win
by any societally-accepted definition.
No way I could be clean.
This was how I learned
the concept of deconstruction of beliefs
as a form of self-preservation.
I had to tear it all down, because by the definitions I had been given
I was disgusting and no one could love me.
No one could love the way I saw myself.
I cannot believe in the pure innocent princess
because the grief that I cannot be her
is overpowering.
I cannot believe in the ruined filthy animal
because the beast chained to the floor
will always wear my face.
I have to be something
else.

Black Void

A black void, full of stars
in which all in existence silently spins.
The universe is cruel, and cold.
So full of things that want to swallow you whole.

Our narratives are always full of bitter ironies
and poetic layers of meaning.

The nothingness, the black void.
It is silent out here. I move, weightless.
No one will ever find me.
There is plenty of time
to think.

Soul-Death

When they who practice reason call it 'unfortunate misunderstanding'
and those who feel remorse call it 'a dark time'
and those who espouse the need for peace call it 'the past'
and 'both sides contributed here'
When they all call it 'forget it, forget it, it's over now'
I call it
Soul-Death.

Mausoleum of Dust

This table has a dusty black tablecloth and is covered
with tumbling vases, wreaths, and baskets of flowers.
The sickly oversweet smell shows that they are old, overripe –
like the body laid out in the parlor, to be frank.
This house is empty, dark and silent.
No one will come through the door to take the corpse somewhere else,
to put the flowers out to decay
and return to the earth.
This is a place of ghosts, and all that is here
will only continue to swell and to wilt.
Nothing will truly decay in this, this mausoleum of dust.
Nothing ever comes here
to rest.

Shining Path

I walked down a shining path
lined with waving boughs.
The sun gazed down upon us all
as I walked along.

I passed a crowd of people
They smiled as they went by.
They opened their mouths and said, wide-eyed
OH GOD HELP WE'RE DYING

I was perturbed, almost disturbed.
Why would someone say something like that?
I looked up and saw other people running
towards me to say hello
except they were moving backwards, fast.
No matter how much I moved forward
I never could close the distance.

The Macabre Club and the Snake Men Servers

The snake man slithered up to me
as I walked through the alley
of the underground city.
He gestured me in through the red angled door,
and I went into a place I had been to before.

I never learned its name, but it was a macabre club
for those not of the mundane variety.
I attracted attention whenever I went in.
Purple stalks and bloody-eyed starts,
fiends of all shapes and types.
The snake men servers slithered around,
black-scaled tails and reptilian eyes.

The menu I never understood, so I never drank anything.
Which was for the best because the one thing I did recognize
was 'mortal's blood.'
It was tapped on-site from tortured souls
to collect the sinful debt they owed.

A demon, seeming human,
except for his endless void eyes
eternally played the piano and sang.
Time was no constraint in this dimension.
I was handed the black and gold saxophone,
and as we played I led the procession
of the entire club dancing as one.

How strange to feel so at home in a place
where there was no one else like me.
A place that, if I was not careful,
I might not leave again.

Coiled Inside

I feel the bitterness and resentment
eating away at me inside.
I feel the weight of it, residing in my mind
coiled there, just biting and biting and biting.

Ancient

Something ancient was unburied
and brought out to the burning light.
A desiccated suffering, decaying, screaming agony
was pulled from the deep cavity in which it was buried
by a stabbing hand that wrenched it out reborn into the world.

Hate and Healing

I did not realize until this moment
that deep down I have always been a creature of hate.

Forever stuck in the moment of when my father
debased me, disgraced me and defaced me,
and then smirked in my face
when the listeners found in his favor.
I was a child, betrayed by my hero.
There was never any closure.

Like the man who, his arm mauled off by wild dogs,
rants and storytells his pain and rage
until his wild eye and hateful tongue
color him bitter and little different from those he was attacked by,
I have spent my life soaking
in a pain-stoked hatred so deep
that those closest to me must at times find it disheartening.
It hurts to see someone you love
so enslaved by the past.

I was never a monster. I did not deserve what was done.
But I have fixated for so long on those who have wronged me
that sometimes I fear that if I were to look in a mirror
I would see something half-changed in front of me.
Hatred-Wendigo. Betrayal-Werewolf. Token and proof that
I allowed the sickness of others to grow as a sickness in me.

I can let this go.
Not all at once, no.
But those friends and lovers and most of all, my father –
they who caused me pain
have their own pain.
Their own betrayals, their own wild dogs.
I can wish them healing, as I have found mine.

I can let this go.

The Ancient Forests

Epochs

It was his time.
Blood dried in place as it ran down the walls,
horrified eyes on cat clock going back and forth;
tick, tock.
tick tock.

Little wrists grabbed and dragged into woods,
weeping willows holding all the misery and shame
the world could not bear to see.
That her tear-filled eyes didn't want them to see.

In this epoch he was a giant and made out of stone and metal.
His arms were held out triumphant and the snarling, sadistic smirk
on his mouth spoke of endless power. Unrivaled dominance.
At least against little girls.

Thousands of years have passed.
Wherever he is, he is likely withered, gray, and corpulent.
The little tree he once felt compelled to torment
and stomp on has since grown into a giant redwood
standing tall and strong, fog draped in an elegant cloak around it.
Even in the stone monster's prime his pride could not have hoped
to hack this tree down. It has surpassed him in every way.

The world is not so large now, or endless.
No longer populated by towering giants
roaring for blood.

It is her time now.

Landfall

I made landfall in a mud-brown swamp at daybreak
filled with filth and corpses.
The small children it was my job to protect laid among them.
I watched myself crumble into rot
and sink into the swamp beside them.

At pitch dark night I walked among a blackened swamp,
oozing with tar and corpses.
Where is this? I cried, but no one answered.
No one answered.

Daybreak my two eyes floated in the swamp.
I saw myself rise, now a nude determined form
that I scarcely recognized.
As they strode out of the muck into the upright
I saw the blackened tree half-expelled from their back.
The glaciers melting have revealed archeological remains
and ancient mummified penguins.
Primordial sleeping bacteria.

Half-exposed, this tree, the roots growing
into me. I could see them all.
The figure reached and pulled, pulled,
this rotten tooth from inside of me.
Washed the ragged, bleeding wounds
with clean water from the mind,
and bandaged them up.

I put these things in a pile and lit them to burn.
They gave little screams, but were converted
into carbon dioxide.
I watched them turn to smoke and dissipate.
I saw the energy convert.

Tarot

I am a queen of grief and grieving,
agony chained round my heart and head.
I am a king of death and dying,
holding in my arms a child dead.
I am a crow flying over the forest,
crying out the bitter truth;
I am a silent owl in the trees below,
already knowing what is true.
Waiting until darkness alights to take flight
and from my beak drop the glowing jewels too.
Jewels that mark a safe path through the forest
at night.

Tower

I spent a very long time locked in a tower
guarded only by dust and decay.
There was no rescuer coming my way.
The outside world didn't know or care that anything was amiss.
Surrounded on every side by miles of trees and silence.
Feeling ruined by wounds and shame I wanted to keep inside.
The rooms always kept dark due to scars on my face and soul
that I wanted to hide.
Keep these mirrors covered, I thought.
This tower is decrepit, consumed by rot.
Like me.
But what actually needed to be done
was to draw back the curtains and allow the sun
to come in.
So it could show me
the way out.

Love of Lives Past

He was definitely the love of my life.
Or at least that life.

But that life is long since gone,
faded away into drying decaying leaves
and the person that life belonged to
is no more.

I will have another love of my life
and hopefully, this time
it will be safe and won't hurt.
I won't be ripped apart like what he did to me
or like, so long ago, what I did to her.

She offered her hand to me.
Two, three, maybe four times
after I had already betrayed her
in my ignorance and self-absorption.
So much strength in that soul
to reach out to me
after everything I had put her through.
I will never know
how a soul could be so powerful.
Over and over
I slammed the door in her face.

The person that hurt her
is long since gone too.
But she never gave the apology she should've.
Never became the person she could've
and though I can see her remains lying against the tree
bleached white resting amongst
decades' worth of leaves
I would give anything

to be able to wake the skeleton
and send it back to the back then.
To do what needed to be done
or, even better,
to undo what I wish she never did.

For F., Again

I have been wandering these woods once more
to ask a pressing question:
Can I try again?
Raising this skeleton up from its bed of dead
leaves at the base of the tree,
leaning it against the trunk.
Can I try again to apologize
to a beautiful soul, inside and out
who I hurt with my own foolishness?

This was 15 years ago, but still –
can I try again?
Draft message saved in my DMs.
But if I reach out to apologize,
will I only make things worse?
What if I only hurt her again?

Shall I just write alone again, then,
as I have always done?
Shall I publish again, then,
in a tome she'll never know of?
Shall I just write it out, again and again,
weathered weary skeleton hand
grasping this pen, writing to a girl
who is likely long since dead,
shed like old skin?
If I were to hand this paper over,
who would it go to?
Who is she now?

I don't deserve
to know.

The Queen in the Forest

The queen sat down on the forest floor,
orange and red leaves in her hair.
The chirping songs of nearby birds as bejeweled
as the gemstones in her golden crown.

Her eyes closed as she took in the breath and murmurings
of the wise old earth.
Her heavy dark dress kept the cold at bay,
while her young brave heart kept the doubts at bay.
Snarling shadows in the distance,
ever ready for the weakness of an unsure heart.

When she rises from the forest floor,
she will be endowed with the surety and strength
a goddess possesses.
A certainty born of communion
with the world of nature and mystery,
a strength of step that accompanies choices made
that are born of a caring heart.
A heart that wants only for the rest of her people,
and all people,
to be able to hear the words of the world
in the silence.

Jeweled Wings

I looked down and saw
my black butterfly wings,
inlaid with vibrant, glittering jewels.

I realized then that I had always been beautiful –
an exotic creature, unique, soft, delicate.
A black swan, an incandescent faerie
fluttering through the midnight woods.

The Castle of Winding Things

In this old, softly crumbling castle
there are winding things.
The corridors, open to the sky
under their protective pillars.
The vines, trellising along the stone walls,
their delicate periwinkle flowers reaching out
to a world they have not given up on,
despite the heavy, sodden rains
and sunless, brooding skies.
The staircases inside, long forgotten
and having forgotten
the sound of human step or hand upon a banister.

Most of all the memories, worn by the only living occupant
in whose mind this place is still pristine and new.
In clouded blue eye and wrinkled brow
she would look frail to any that would see her.
But she will never die.
She is as old as this castle is, as undying,
as wild.
She braids collected flowers into her hair
and waits for the old days to return.

Apology, Finally

I did it. I apologized to her.
To one I loved so long ago
and wronged with my ignorance
and selfishness.

I don't know if she read it.
If she saw it or even received it.
All of those settings with Message Request
folders and whatnot.
But I said what needed to be said
and I have faith that if she is meant to see it
the universe will deliver it so.
If not, then it will just mean
that it was too little
too late.

Either way, the journey
through these particular woods
is over.

I think of all the apologies that I am due
that I will likely never receive.
All of the situations in which
I will have to cultivate my own closure
and peace.

But at least I have given an apology
that I owed.

Of Storms and the Sea

Pressed Flowers and the Sea Serpent

White and rose-pink flowers, dried and pressed.
The raging maw
of the sea serpent.
Writhing and roaring in the waves,
still and pensive in between the pages.

Will anyone see it;
has anyone ever seen it.
The fragility and the ferocity.
The sickly-pallored, luminous-eyed
countenance of the medium.
She's a powerful one.
Swirling dead leaves stirred up
and echoing voices out beyond the mirrors.
It all resides on the planet inside,
the inner landscape in which
everything makes sense.

Everything outside of it is a goddamn mess.
It's absolutely insane.
Its unyielding disinterest
in the thoughts and feelings of those observing it.
Its cold lack of concern or care
for the condition of those experiencing it.

Does anyone see any of it? The planet inside?
This mysterious, tumultuous, crystal-and-stone world?
The purple trees, the embodied deities
of Love, Betrayal, Self-Loathing, and Fear?
Where Depression has long held a comfortable seat
at the head of this regal table?
Can anyone hear the rainbow birds
or see the reflection of their jeweled wings on the wall?
From where the sun shines in?

Can anyone see any of this?
Hear any of it?
Or is this giant sea serpent roaring
into an empty abyss, a closed cover
and are the delicate flowers pressed
into a handmade book, another
gift that, aside from one page,
will never be looked at again?

To the outside world, does any of this exist?
This poem asks, "Will anyone ever find this?"

A Fisher by the Sea

I saw a fisher by the sea.
He was clothed in white.
He was waiting, wrapped and cold,
and had been through the night.
He was always there.

Lonely and drawn, his face was always tired.
He was always staring down into the sea.
But one day his countenance suddenly brightened up;
there was a gold-plated fish in the water.

His joy was a warm delight
as he reached down into the sea.
I was smiling as wide as he
until the fish's teeth suddenly bared
and it swallowed his hand.
He screamed and screamed and screamed.

After that day I always saw the fisher by the sea
in rust-stained white robes with his head down,
bandages wrapped around the loss.
I watched him grow old and stand on the shore
as he watched the young people jump and play
amidst the waves and rocks.
He didn't look in the water anymore.

One day while he was walking, lost in thought,
I think he realized he'd stepped too close to the edge.
He looked quickly left and saw
an all-white fish peering up from the water.
He looked and looked,
and then remembered his hand.
He turned from the white fish in the sea

and left forevermore that same shore
wrapped in robes and grief.

The Mermaids and the Moon

I will tell you about the time
I met the mermaids.

It was night, but an illuminated night
due to the impressive moon.
It cast its light over the murmuring waves
and the island in their center.
The island being mostly comprised
of the cave.

I had already run from the juveniles.
They appeared as elegant young women at first.
But like most young predators they were ravenously hungry
and before long their screeches and howls echoed off the walls
of the cave and I ran, and alternately splashed, through the maze.
Their real bodies were solid like seals, covered in sharp spikes and
stripes.
Their heads were mostly comprised of sharp teeth, quivering crests,
and demanding eyes.
Their fins still small and undeveloped.
They were slow on land but dangerously fast in water.
As I ran I found the occasional scrap of flesh, fragment of bone,
all that was left from their voracious appetites.

But when I came out of the other side of the cave
I saw Her – the Full-Grown.
A giant white sea creature, appearing as between
dragon and serpent.
Her fins were long, and elegant,
and she could hover in the sky.
And when she looked at me,
I heard her speak in my mind.

She told me to not mind the Children,

that at this age all they could think about
was their need to eat.
She said they were only a few centuries old,
whereas she had been here since the dinosaurs or so.
She lived eternally here, with the moon.
This was the moon's true home.

So on that evening I met not just
mermaids, nor just an ancient, wise observer,
their Mother;
I got to truly witness the moon.
To see it much closer up, and much larger, too,
resting in its bed above a timeless sea dreaming.

The Storm

I used to be on the ship, battling
the storm-churning waves.
For the past several years I have sat on the calm beach,
looking back on those hard days.
But another change has also taken place.
I know now that, if the world should need it
and I should stand up and wade into the sea,
I will feel the shift as I become the lightning, the ocean roar,
the giant sea dragon calling the storm
and I will send corrupt and twisted ships
crashing down into the waves
to sink to the ocean floor.

Two Souls Out at Sea

We were two lost souls thrashing about in the sea
who happened to grab onto each other accidentally.
I thought he was the one, that I had finally found
what I was looking for.
I didn't understand that what I needed was the shore.
And of course he ended up putting my head under the water,
though I suppose he didn't mean to.
What else is going to happen
when two people are stranded out at sea
and struggling to keep afloat?

Hollow of the River

Someday I will love again.
But never like that. Never in that way.
A new love will have its own course, its own feeling.
But it will never feel like that.

I will always carry the hollow of that river inside my heart
where once love was coursing through it, rushing and roaring,
pure and beautiful and destructive and devouring.
In the scars along its banks and the torn, ragged trees
will be the memories of when it jumped its banks
and destroyed huge swaths of me.

Things grow back. Trees return,
birds begin to sing once more.

Someday I will love again.
But that mausoleum will always stand,
an empty hollow of what was once a river
attended by ruined stumps of trees.
A monument to the love that came,
and the love that destroyed.

Consciousness

I found Consciousness as I held my gutted entrails
in the wake of my father's blade.
I Awoke in the wake of a soulmate's curled hands
ripping away sections of my flesh.

I am so much stronger for having navigated through
to the eye of these bitter storms of agony.
I have found Awareness and Truth
through suffering.

There is no one to search for. No one to impress.
And I have nothing to lose because I have already lost it all,
only to find that I never had anything in the first place.
There is nothing left to draw back from
in horror.

I have nothing to fear from the biting winds, the raging storms,
for I have become them.
I dance with the lightning and sing with the thunder.

Sunset Over the Sea

I'm not good or bad.
Friendly or aloof.
Laid-back or dramatic.
I'm not any of the terms that people
could come up with to describe me,
nor am I the limited things
that I think myself to be.
I am so much more than that.

I'm so much more than any adjective,
could never be contained by any collection of nouns.
I am the churning, frothing waves as they splash
over ancient rocks onto the smoothed shore.
I am so much more.

I reflect on pain, how we've all felt it and caused it.
I used to think that was all life had in store.
A monotonous recounting and contemplation
of all the bad things that had happened before,
only to then go out and experience some more.

There is a difference between how you feel
and what you are.
When drowning in my emotions
I am held in such a small container,
the sealed jar lost out at sea.
When the real truth is
I am the entire sea.
Emotions, traits, past experiences
are just transient, individual facets of me.
And the world.

And if I am to be a feeling,
for any length of time,

let's pick a better one to personify.
Let me be the feeling of ethereal timelessness
that comes from watching the sun set
over the sea.
Or the rushing sense of renewal that arrives
as the everlasting waves crash onto the shore,
and then ebb back away into the ocean once more.
Let me be that feeling of a beginning
that never
ends.

Mistress of Her Vessel

She is the mistress of her vessel,
gliding silently out to sea
in the descending twilight.

As the night descends you may see her
sail off the edge of the ocean
into the gentle starlight.

Free from the constraints of time and space,
she will guide her craft onward
into the eternal midnight.

The Wires

I stood back from the wires and watched the storylines unfold.
A betrayal. A sacrifice. An alliance on shaky ground.
A euphoric victory and a dystopian breakdown.
I heard the sizzling and crackling as they traveled down the wires.

A spilled bottle of black ink
blossomed across the white canvas.
I watched the stories swell like waves across the page,
split and delineate into individual curving lines.
Each tale separate yet interconnected with the rest.

A small weathered boat trying to go out to a grayscale sea.
Loaded down with heavy boxes, filled to overflowing
with broken and tired things.
As I stood on the shore, I let my tired hands finally unfold
and released that which was ready to leave so long ago.

The peace I found when I realized
I don't need to be plugged into the machinery.
I don't need to write out the ink.
I can step back from it all, and the cacophony
of laughing, weeping, screaming voices
can fade away down the page.
Can be carried away down the wires.

The relief that swept over me to know
that the little white boat
can become smaller and smaller
as it goes out to sea.
Finally disappearing
in the distance.

ABOUT THE AUTHOR

Michaela Belmont is an award-winning author from California with a BA in sociology and an MA in English and creative writing. After spending many years struggling with the pain of existence she decided to make art from it instead. She writes about trauma, healing, and the spirit realms.

LEARN MORE

website: michaelabelmont.com
instagram: @michaela.belmont

www.ingramcontent.com/pod-product-compliance
Lightning Source LLC
Chambersburg PA
CBHW020427010526
44118CB00010B/460